TOY FADS

by Beth Dvergsten Stevens

COVER-TO-COVER BOOKS

Perfection Learning®

Cover Design: Michelle Glass
Inside Layout: Katherine Zeph
Photography: Michael Aspengren

DEDICATION

For all kids who like to try the newest fads. Especially for
my daughters, the enthusiastic fad queens at our house. Thanks
for the memories. Thanks also to Marcy A. for her recollections.

Cover images: ©CORBIS royalty-free—legos™ and Slinky; ©2001 Hasbro, Inc. Used
with permission—G. I. Joe®; FRISBEE® is a registered trademark of WHAM-O,
Inc.—Frisbee disc; ™ & © 2001 Saban—Mighty Morphin Power Ranger

Illustration: Mike Aspengren p. 32

Credits: ©Bettman/CORBIS pp. 13, 14, 40 (top), 53; ©Philip Gould/CORBIS
p. 17; ©Lynda Richardson/CORBIS p. 18; ©Roger Ressmeyer/CORBIS p. 22; ©Karl
Weatherly/CORBIS p. 35; ©Owen Franken/CORBIS p. 41

ArtToday (some images copyright www.arttoday.com); Corel Professional Photos
pp. 10 (left), 26, 55; Corel.com p. 20; some images ISMI® Master Clip Art; ©CORBIS
royalty-free pp. 3, 40 (bottom), 49; ©RUSS troll doll p. 33; Nerf® title page, p. 38
©2001 Hasbro, Inc. Used with permission; G. I Joe® pp. 27, 48 ©2001 Hasbro, Inc.
Used with permission; Transformer pp. 28–29 Transformers are manufactured under
license from Takara Co., Ltd.; Silly Putty and The Real Solid Liquid are registered
trademarks of Binney & Smith, used with permission pp. 23, 24 (Marc Thies
stretching Silly Putty); Mighty Morphin Power Ranger™ & © 2001 Saban p. 30

Play Doh®, Spirograph® and Twister® & ©2001 Hasbro, Inc. Used with permission.
Furby® & ©2001 Tiger Electronics., Ltd.

CONTENTS

CHAPTER 1

A HISTORY OF TOY FADS

The new boy was from California. He held a shiny red board with wheels. Everyone watched him. They wondered what he was going to do.

The boy stood at the top of a slope on the playground. He set the board down. He carefully stood up on it. Then he rode the board down the slope. He held his arms out for balance. He looked just like a surfer!

Nobody had ever seen anything like it. Everybody cheered! This was the first skateboard in town.

Everyone wanted to try it. Everyone wanted to get a skateboard. Local stores ordered them. Children stood in line to buy them.

Soon, kids rode skateboards all over town. It was 1964. Skateboarding was a brand-new toy fad in Minnesota. The sport was already popular in California.

WHAT IS A FAD?

A fad is something new and exciting. A fad toy is fun! It must be special in some way too. Maybe it's very odd. Maybe it's cute. Maybe it goes faster or higher than other toys. Maybe it just has a funny name. For some reason, the toy catches on. It becomes popular very quickly.

Many toy fads have come and gone. Hula hoops and Frisbee® discs were fads. So were Slinkys, Superballs, and Silly Putty. Furbys® and Floam were fads. Beanie Babies, yo-yos, and Pogs were fads too. All of these toys seemed special and new. Even their names were fun to say.

How Do Fads Begin?

Some toys are brand-new ideas or inventions. They have never been made before.

Silly Putty was a new invention. But it was made by mistake. It was supposed to be a new kind of rubber material. It made a better toy instead.

Pogs and Slinkys seemed like new inventions too. But Pogs started out as bottle caps. Slinkys were just metal springs. They became big fads when inventors turned them into toys. Kids liked to play with them. And they didn't cost much money.

Other fads are old toys. But they seem new and different. They've been changed in some way. The changes made the toys more fun.

Hoops, flying discs, and balls are very old toys. But someone made them new and better. The new hoops and discs were colorful. They were made of plastic. The new balls bounced very high.

The toy names were new too. Hula hoops, Frisbee® discs, and Superballs sounded like fun toys. All of a sudden these old toys became popular again.

When a fad toy is new, children play with it all the time. They take it to school and parties. They practice using it. They learn how to do tricks.

But after a year or two, the craze dies down. Kids find other toys to buy. The fad toys lie forgotten in toy boxes or closets. They fade away as fast as they started.

WHERE DO TOY FADS BEGIN?

Many fads begin on the West Coast, in states like California. Others begin in eastern states such as Connecticut or New York. Fads move quickly across the United States. People see them when they travel. They see them on television, in magazines, or in movies. Toy companies advertise the toys too. Fad toys are popular because they are different and interesting.

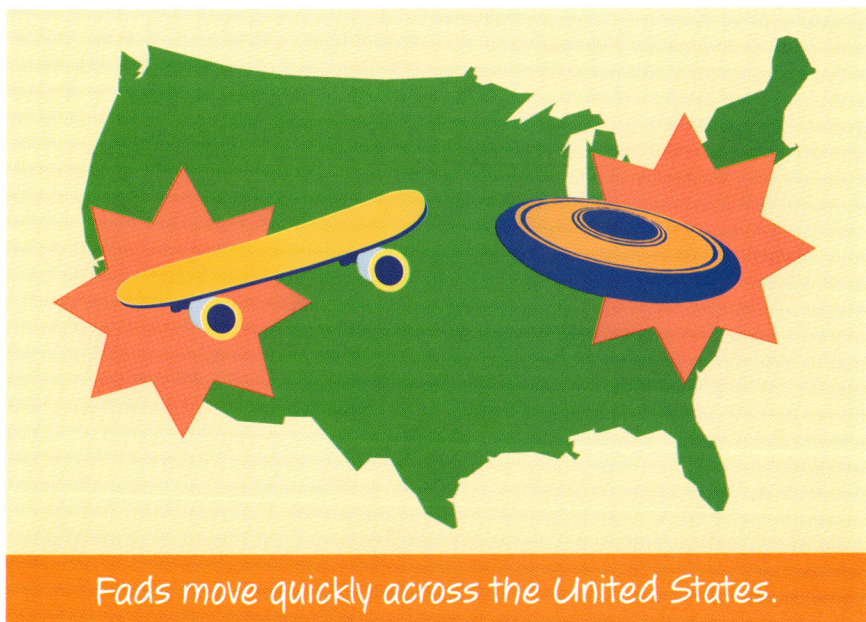

Fads move quickly across the United States.

WHERE DO FADS GO?

Some fads disappear. Children don't want the toys anymore. So factories stop making them. Stores stop selling them. The Pogs fad is an example of one that died quickly.

Other fads stay alive. Children still like these toys. So factories keep making them. Stores keep selling them to new generations of children. These fad toys have turned into classics. Hula hoops, Frisbee® discs, Legos, and Slinkys are classics now.

It's hard to predict which new toys will become fads. And who knows which fads will become classics? But each fad toy is fun and exciting. And when it has a fun name, it is even better!

HOW HAVE TOYS CHANGED?

A hundred years ago, toys were simple. Then the world changed. Inventors thought of new ideas. Many new toys were invented after World War II. But old toys and new toys are alike in many ways. Children still like to do the same things. Compare old toys with the modern toys.

Years ago, kids played with puzzles.

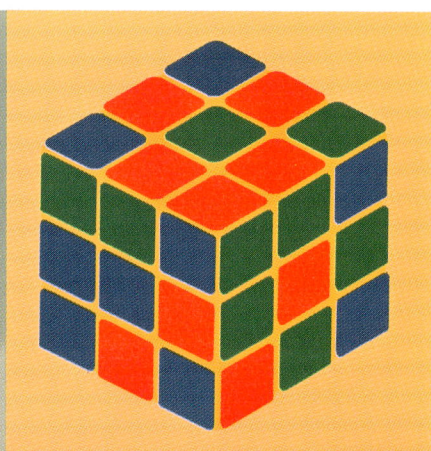

The matching toy fad is Rubik's Cube® (1974).

KIDS BEGAN PLAYING WITH	THE MATCHING TOY FAD IS
mud, clay	Silly Putty (1950), Floam (1994)
rag dolls, Raggedy Ann and Andy (1915)	Cabbage Patch Kids (1983), Beanie Babies (1993)
tin and lead soldiers	plastic action figures such as G. I. Joe (1964), Superman, Transformers® (1984), Teenage Mutant Ninja Turtles (1988), Mighty Morphin Power Rangers™ (1994)
paper dolls, cornhusk dolls	Barbie (1959)
chalk, pencils, paper	Etch A Sketch (1960), Spirograph® (1965)
pie pans, cookie tin lids	Frisbee® disc (1959)
wooden or metal hoops	plastic hula hoops (1958)
leather or rubber balls	Nerf balls (1970), Superballs (1966), Hacky Sacks (1983)
real pets such as dogs, cats	virtual pets such as Tamagotchi (1997), Furby (1998)
scooters, skate coasters	skateboards (1961)
puzzles	Instant Insanity (1968), Rubik's Cube (1974)
wood blocks	Erector sets (1914), Legos (1949)

2

CHAPTER

TOYS TO SPIN, THROW, OR BOUNCE

HULA HOOPS 1958

A hoop is a simple toy. It's an old toy too. People have played with hoops since ancient Greek and Roman times. They rolled wooden or metal hoops on the ground. They tossed hoops into the air.

Hoops were used for exercise too. In the 1950s, children in Australia twirled bamboo hoops in gym class. Then two American men saw the hoops. They got an idea. They made a new kind of hoop toy for American children.

First they made the hoops from wood. They suggested that children twirl them around their waists.

Then the men made the hoops from plastic. They called them *hula hoops*. Something amazing happened. Children went crazy for the new hoops! It was 1958 when the hula hoop fad started.

People twirled the hoops in backyards and parks, on playgrounds, and at parties. Contests were held. People counted the number of times they could spin the hoops without stopping. They twirled many hoops at the same time. They learned tricks.

The hula hoop is often called the *Granddaddy of American Fads*. In just a few months, 25 million hula hoops were sold!

It seemed like everyone was twirling them.

Hula hoops today are fancier. Some even make noise. But all hula hoops are fun to twirl.

MARCY'S STORY

Marcy was nine years old when she got her first hula hoop. She was so excited! She ran into the backyard and tried twirling the hoop around her waist. It was hard to do. But she practiced and practiced. The more she twirled it, the easier it became. Before long, she could wiggle her hips just the right speed.

She learned to twirl it 100 times without stopping. She could spin it around her neck, shoulders, waist, and knees before it hit the ground.

She and her friends learned tricks too. They jumped through rolling hoops. They threw them with a spin and watched the hoops roll back to them.

But after a year or two, Marcy's hula hoop sat in her closet while she and her friends played other games.

THE FRISBEE® DISC NAME

This toy had many names. But Frisbee® disc is the name that stuck. Students yelled "Frisbie" to warn people when a flying disc was coming their way. Frisbie was also the name on the pie pans they threw. When Wham-O heard the name, they thought it was perfect. But they spelled it F-r-i-s-b-e-e instead.

FRISBEE® DISCS 1959

Flying discs aren't new. In ancient Greece, men threw them for sport. The early Olympic athletes tested their throwing skills with a discus. Some metal discs were weapons too.

But a plastic Frisbee® disc is light and colorful. It was a huge fad in the late 1950s. And today, it's still popular with people of all ages.

The disc is round and flat. It's shaped like a pie pan. In fact, the first discs were metal pie pans!

The Frisbie Baking Company in Connecticut made pies. One day in the early 1900s, someone tossed an empty pie pan into the air. It sailed toward a friend. The friend caught it. That started a new game at the Frisbie Company.

The factory workers played catch with the pie pans outside. Some college students saw the game. It looked like fun. They started playing catch with the pie pans too. The game quickly spread to other colleges.

College students played with other flat discs too. They used metal lids from large cookie tins. They used paint-can lids and flat baskets. Some even used phonograph records.

Then in 1946, two World War II pilots made discs from something new. It was hard plastic. They called these discs Whirlo Ways and Flyin' Saucers. They showed their toys to people in California. But they didn't sell very many.

One of the men decided to make the toy better. He used softer plastic. The new disc flew well.

A toy company saw it. They liked it. So they bought it. They called it a "Pluto Platter."

Even dogs play with the discs!

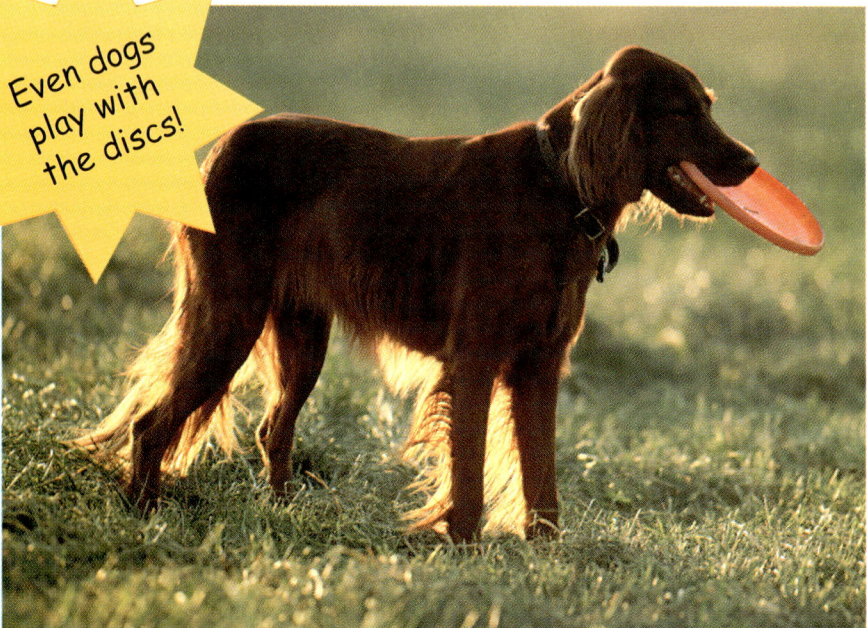

It seemed like a flying saucer. In 1957, they started making and selling them.

A year later, they made the discs even better. And they changed the name to Frisbee® disc.

Before long, the Frisbee® disc fad caught on. New games were invented. Contests were held and clubs were formed.

Playing games with these discs is a very popular sport today. Even dogs play with the discs!

SUPERBALLS
1966

People have played with balls for a very long time. But the Superball was a great new invention. It could bounce sky-high!

In the 1960s, a chemist invented something called Zectron. It was very bouncy.

A toy company started making balls from Zectron. They were the bounciest balls kids had ever seen.

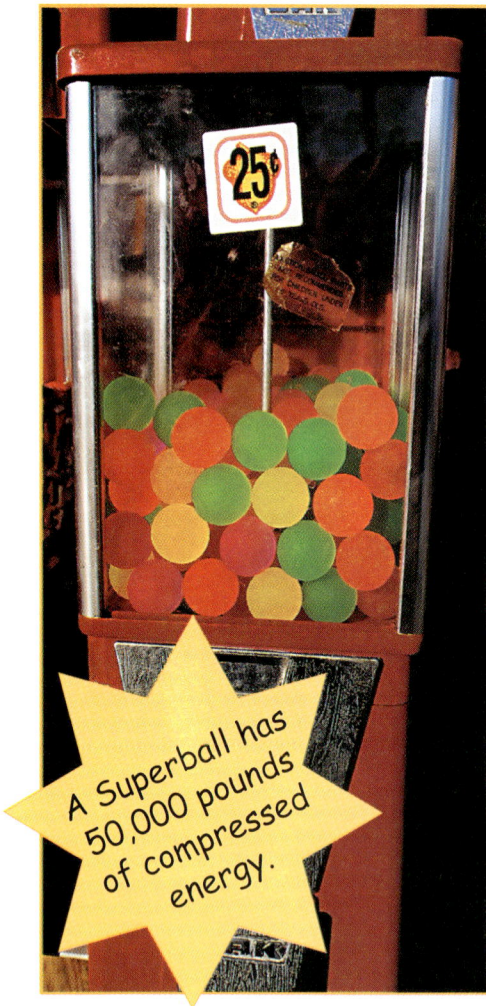

A Superball has 50,000 pounds of compressed energy.

Everyone rushed to buy them. Superballs became very popular. Twenty million balls were sold in the 1960s.

The ball's label said it had 50,000 pounds of compressed energy. That's a lot of power! In Australia, it was too much power. It caused an accident.

Salesmen were showing the new Superballs. A big Superball fell from the twenty-third floor of a tall hotel. It bounced back up 15 floors. Then it went down again. It landed on a parked car. The car was wrecked. But the ball was fine.

CHAPTER 3

TOYS THAT STRETCH AND BEND

SLINKYS
1945

A Slinky is just a big spring. But it's a spring that does tricks.

Slinkys didn't start out as toys. They were supposed to be tools.

During World War II, an engineer named Richard James had an important project. He was trying to make better springs for ships. The springs would help level boats when they sailed on rough water.

One day, Mr. James knocked one big spring to the floor. It bounced. Then it moved end over end. It kept moving. It looked like it was walking.

Mr. James showed the spring to his wife. They laughed at it. They tried it on a stairway. The spring walked down the steps.

Mr. and Mrs. James decided the spring would be a fun toy. So they showed it to people in Philadelphia.

These people thought it was fun to watch. Mr. James and his wife sold 400 Slinkys that day! That was the start of the Slinky business.

You can still buy metal Slinkys today. You can buy plastic ones or ones that look like pets too.

SILLY PUTTY 1950

original Silly Putty packaging

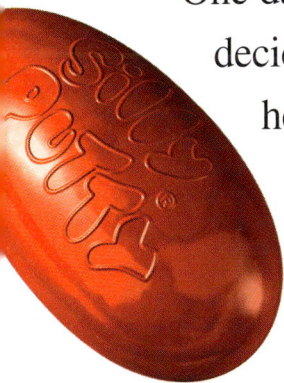

James Wright was a chemical engineer. He was trying to invent something to replace real rubber. But he made something else instead.

He mixed boric acid with silicon oil. The solid mixture bounced like rubber. It stretched like rubber. But it snapped and broke. It looked like goop. He called it "Gooey Gupp."

Gupp samples were sent to engineers around the United States. They looked at it. But no one could figure out how to use it.

One day, Peter Hodgson saw it. He decided putty would be a great toy. So he bought some of it.

Mr. Hodgson split the putty into small pieces. It was close to Easter. So he put the pieces into plastic eggs. He named it *Silly Putty*. He said it was a real solid liquid.

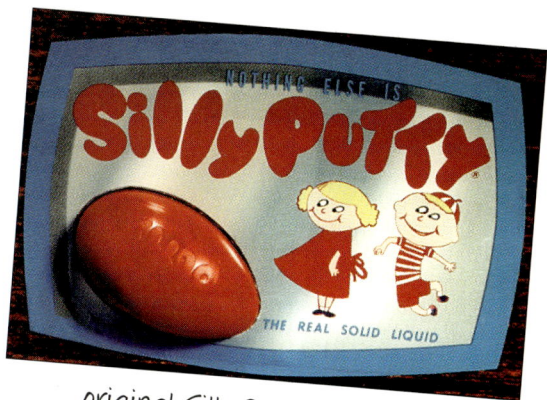

Some stores agreed to sell the new toy. But not many people bought it.

Then a New York magazine advertised it. Soon Mr. Hodgson had 25,000 orders!

Children really liked Silly Putty. Within five years, he sold 32 million pieces of it. Kids still like it today.

LIGHTS, CAMERA, ACTION FIGURES!

Long ago, children played with small toy soldiers and horses. In ancient Egypt and Rome, they played with clay ones. In Europe, some toy soldiers were carved from wood. Still others were made from metals like lead, tin, and silver.

The toy soldiers looked real. They wore uniforms with caps or helmets. Knights and infantry soldiers marched into battle. Many were painted.

Some soldiers rode horses. Others carried weapons or drums. The toys were small enough to hold.

For centuries, children set up battles and galloped their toy horses. Their soldiers bravely fought their enemies.

Today, stores sell buckets of small plastic soldiers. But another toy is more popular. It's the plastic action figure. Action figures are heroes who save the day.

Hasbro's G. I. Joe® brand was the first action figure. He was made in 1964. He had joints so he could bend and move. He was almost 12 inches tall.

G. I. Joe action figures were based on the Army, Navy, Air Force, and Marines. Each one wore a uniform and dog tags. And each one had special accessories.

But the toy company was worried. Would boys like these "movable soldiers"?

Yes! They loved the new toys. They posed the soldiers in battle. They changed their uniforms. They made up battle plans. G. I. Joe action figures were a hit.

Before long, G. I. Joe figures had vehicles and more accessories.

Soon other action figures were created. Some were the same size as G. I. Joe 12" figures. Others were small enough to fit into a pocket or hand.

G. I. Joe

Transformer

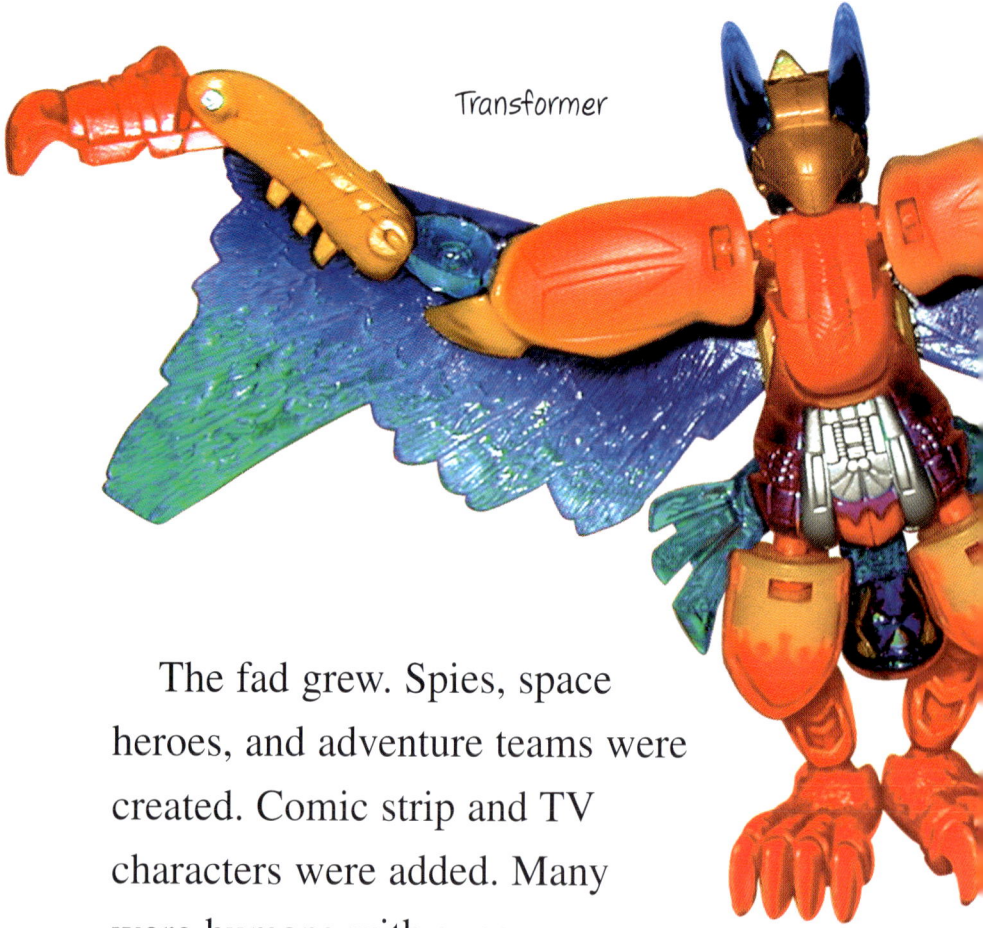

The fad grew. Spies, space
heroes, and adventure teams were
created. Comic strip and TV
characters were added. Many
were humans with superpowers,
such as Batman, Superman, Captain Action,
and Spiderman. Teams of figures like X-Men,
Masters of the Universe, and Mighty Morphin
Power Rangers joined the others. Not all the
heroes were human. Some were aliens. Others
were part animal, part human.

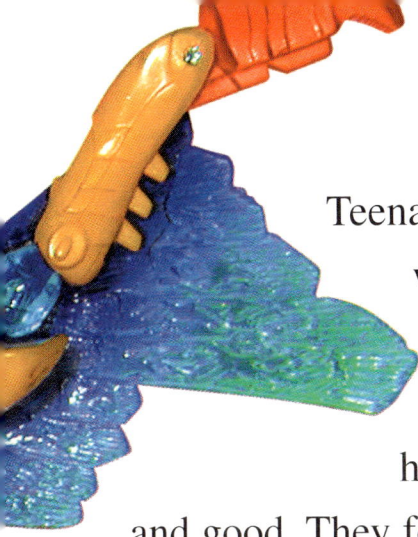

Teenage Mutant Ninja Turtles were popular in the late 1980s. They were turtles who were part human. They were brave and good. They fought crime with ninja power and humor.

Some figures transformed, or changed into something else. These figures were like puzzles. Many were vehicles that turned into fierce robots.

Action-figure fads changed as the world did. When new movies were made, new action figures were made too. Some of these toys didn't last long. But others, like the G. I. Joe brand and Superman, have stayed popular for a long time.

Many different fad characters have come and gone. But one thing is always the same. The good guys fight the bad guys. And the good guys usually save the day!

The good
guys usually
save the day!

Mighty Morphin
Power Ranger

HERE TODAY, GONE TOMORROW?

FADS WITH SHORT LIVES

Some fads were popular for a very short time. Then they disappeared. People forgot about them.

CLACKERS

Clackers were two balls on a string. They bounced off each other. They made a clacking noise. Players tried to keep them moving for a long time. But sometimes the plastic balls broke. This toy fad didn't last.

POGS

Pogs were cardboard bottle caps for games and trading. In the mid-1990s, kids collected and traded Pogs everywhere. Each Pog was colorful. "Slammers" were made from metal or plastic. Players stacked the Pogs into a pile. A player dropped a slammer on the pile. That player took every Pog that flipped over on his turn.

FLOAM

This goopy mixture was fun to handle and mold. It came in bright colors. It was cool and bumpy to touch. Special toys were used to mold it.
Play Doh® is still popular, but Floam is gone.

Fads with Second Lives

Some toys get a second chance. These toys become popular again with a different generation of children.

These odd-looking dolls with wild, colorful hair were a craze in the 1960s. The first ones were four inches tall. Later they came in all sizes. In the 1980s, they became a minifad again.

Troll Dolls

Yo-Yos

Yo-yos are wood or plastic discs that spin down and up on strings. This fad is like its name. This toy comes back again and again. It is an ancient toy that became popular in the 1920s. After the Depression, the fad died. In the 1960s, it came back. It was popular again in the late 1990s. Every so often, kids rediscover this toy.

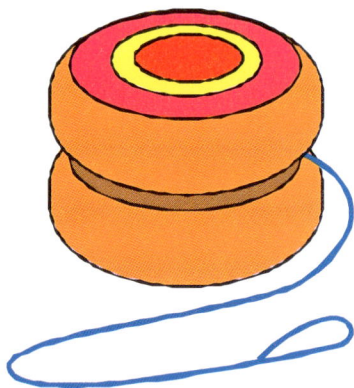

Tops

These toys spin on a point. They are ancient toys. New models and materials make the tops seem fun again. In the 1950s and 60s, many fun tops appeared. Some made loud sounds. Some had friction motors to spin fast. In the 1990s, tops became popular again.

These surfboards for sidewalks were big in 1960s. By 1970, the fad faded. The craze came back in the 1980s with better boards and exciting skateboard parks.

HOW DO PEOPLE FIND OUT ABOUT NEW TOYS?

To become a fad, people have to see a toy and want it. They become aware of new toys in several ways.

Show-and-sell is one of the easiest ways to get people interested in toys. Toys are displayed and demonstrated in public.

- The inventors of the hula hoop demonstrated the hoops in parks and on playgrounds. They let children try them. They gave away free hoops to children who could spin them.

- Company employees played with Etch A Sketches on airplanes when they traveled. People saw the toys and wanted to try them.

- The inventor of Silly Putty took it to parties. People played with it. They thought it was great!

News of new toys is often spread by word of mouth. If people like the new toys, they tell other people about them. Those people tell more people. The toys become popular that way.

Media advertising is one of the best ways to reach many people. For example, when people saw the hula hoop on television, they all wanted it. The ads made these toys look like fun. Children asked their parents to buy them.

SOME FADS LIVE ON

NERF® BALLS 1970

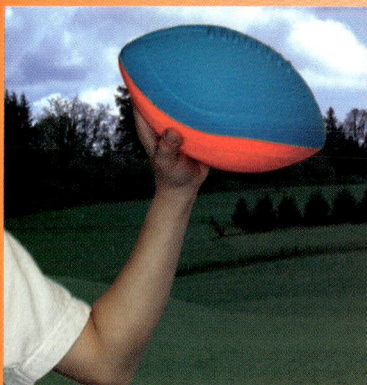

No one knew these fads would still be favorites today.

Kids could play with these soft, spongy balls inside. Since they are soft, they don't cause damage like harder balls. Parents like that. Today, many different Nerf toys fill shelves in toy stores.

TWISTER®
1966

Twister was a popular game of twists and movement for parties. Today, people of all ages play the game. It's still fun.

ETCH A SKETCHES
1960

Etch A Sketch drawing boards were best-selling Christmas gifts in 1960. The factory could hardly fill all the orders by December 25. People still like to draw pictures with them today.

MAGIC 8 BALLS
1950s

These balls "tell" fortunes. Players ask questions. Then a Magic 8 Ball "answers" through a tiny window on the bottom. It can't really tell fortunes, but it's a fun toy anyway.

POGO STICKS 1924

Over the years, the pogo stick fad has faded and come back several times. Kids like to jump and test their balance on the bouncy sticks.

LEGOS 1949

These plastic interlocking blocks have never lost their popularity. More blocks and building sets can be found today than ever before.

BEANIE BABIES
1993

Kids and adults collect these small beanbag animals. Hundreds have been made. The company "retires" some animals each year. That makes them hard to find in stores. But half the fun is hunting for them.

MAKE IT AND PLAY!

HOMEMADE FUNNY PUTTY

Make your own putty. Divide it into small wads. Store each one in a plastic egg, just like the real Silly Putty.

USES

- Stretch it, squeeze it, or tear it.
- Wad it up and bounce it.
- Let it "drip" off your hand.
- Press it on black and white newspaper print.
- Draw pictures with a pencil. Press putty over pencil marks to pick them up. Then stretch the pictures out of shape.

NEEDS

- 1/2 teaspoon powdered borax
- 1/4 cup warm water
- 1/2 cup white glue
- 1/4 cup cold water

STEPS

1. In a bowl, mix the borax with the warm water. Stir until it's dissolved.

2. Put the glue into a large, disposable plastic container.

3. Pour the cold water into the glue. Mix well.

4. Pour the borax and water mixture into the glue mixture. Watch carefully. Stir well until a lump of putty forms around your spoon.

5. Knead the putty with hands for a few minutes until it is less sticky. Work in all of the liquid. Then let it rest a few minutes.

6. Store putty in an airtight plastic container. Wash your hands well after using the putty.

Decorated Flying Discs

Make your own flying disc from a metal pie pan. Then play "frisbie" with it, just as the first players did.

Tips

1. Fly the disc in a large open area away from streets.

2. Don't play during the hottest part of the day.

3. Choose a calm day. If it's windy outside, play another game.

4. Keep your fingernails short.

5. Try different grips.

6. The faster the disc spins, the better it will fly.

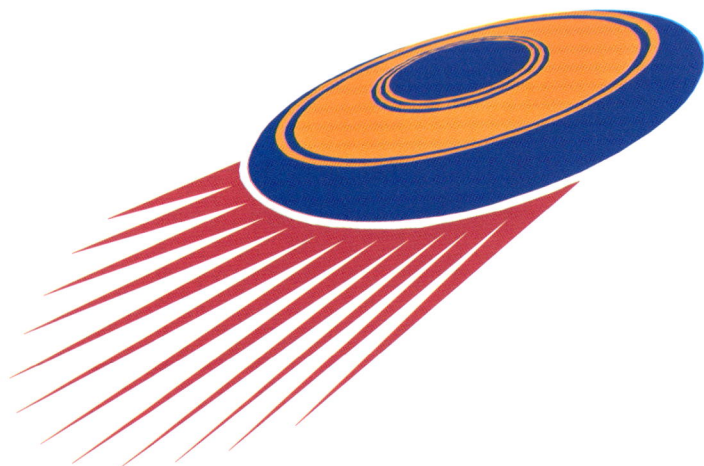

NEEDS

- metal pie pan
- colorful electrical tapes
- scissors
- stickers
- opaque paint markers

STEPS

1. Press strips of tape around the slanted edge of the pie pan. Stretch the tape slightly so it lies flat.

2. Put stickers on pan bottom. Space them evenly so the pie pan is balanced.

3. Finish decorating with paint markers.

OTHER HOMEMADE FLYING DISCS

- Use a bamboo paper plate holder instead of the pie pan. Thread colorful yarn through a big, blunt needle. Weave the yarn in and out of the plate holder edges.

- Substitute the lid from a five-quart plastic ice cream bucket for the pie pan. Decorate the top and edges of the plastic lid with electrical tape or paint markers.

Flying Disc Target Games

The game of disc golf was invented in 1937. It was called "Disc Scaling." Players tried to "putt" their discs into different baskets on a course. Make your own simple target games.

- **Chalk Targets:** Draw large circles on a driveway with sidewalk chalk. Try to land your disc in the circles.

- **Hoop Targets:** Hang a hula hoop in a tree. Stand ten feet away. Throw your disc through the hoop. As your aim gets better, step farther away from the hoop.

- **Disc Golf:** Set up several targets. Count the number of throws it takes to get from one target to the other, just like golf. The lowest score wins.

8

CHAPTER

FUN FAD TRIVIA

FUNNY FAD NAMES

- Silly Putty was called "Gooey Gupp" by its inventor.

- The Frisbee® disc was called a "Pluto Platter" in 1955. Flying discs had many other names such as "Flyin' Saucer," "Space Saucer," "Mars Platter," and "Magic Saucer."

- A reflyer is a Frisbee® disc made of recycled plastic.

- Hula hoops were almost called "Twirl-a-Hoops" or "Swing-a-Hoops." But the inventors named them after the Hawaiian hula dance instead. Twirlers have to swivel their hips, just like hula dancers.

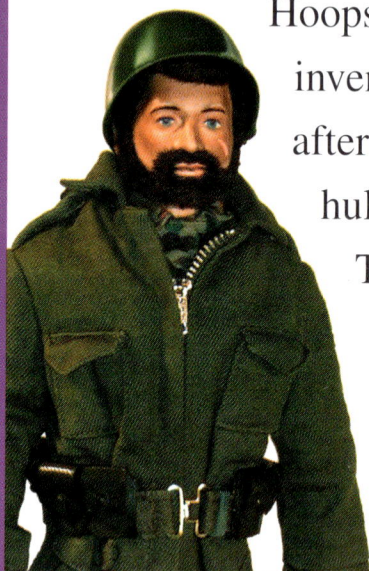

G. I. JOE

G. I. Joe means "Government-Issue Joe," from a 1945 war movie.

SLINKY

The slinky was almost called "Slither."

- A hula hoop is called "Haru Hoopu" in Japan.

- Pogs were named for a juice drink made in Hawaii. The drink was made from passion fruit, orange juice, and guava juice. POG was printed on each bottle cap. Kids played a game with the paper bottle caps. So the game and game pieces were called "Pogs."

- "The Twist" was a dance that started in the 1960s. Its inventor got the idea from the hula hoop fad.

- Pokémon games and trading cards became a fad in the late 1990s. Kids tried to collect every card. Pokémon was everywhere.

- The earliest discs were everyday items from metal covers off cans of cookies and chips to paint-can lids to woven baskets, serving trays, and old phonograph records. People used anything flat and round.

SKATEBOARD

In 1950, a bored surfer nailed roller skates to a water ski. This was the first skateboard.

- Frisbee® discs have gone into space with astronauts. And they have been tossed off the Himalayan mountains.

- Every G. I. Joe figure has a scar on its right cheek. It also has a factory mistake. One thumbnail is on the wrong side of the thumb. The company decided to keep the mistake so Joe was special.

- Playing with Hacky Sacks was a "foot fad" in the 1980s. Players had to keep the small bean-filled ball in the air. But they couldn't use their hands.

- In 1967, the hula hoop fad was fading. So the company put little balls inside their hoops. The new hoops made a shoop-shoop sound. The hula hoop seemed new again. It became a minifad.

AMAZING NUMBERS AND RECORDS

- When hula hoops were most popular, the company made 20,000 hoops every day. In less than two years, they had sold 100 million.

- In 1999, one woman twirled 82 hula hoops at the same time.

- In 1994, a woman threw a Frisbee® disc 447 feet to set a world record. In 1998, the men's world record was 693 feet. How far can you throw one?

90 HOURS!

In 1987, a college student twirled her hula hoop for 90 hours!

2,000 PEOPLE!

In 1990, about 2,000 people twirled hula hoops at the same time in Canada.

Mimi Jordan, 10, drinks milk and holds a sandwich while hula-hooping and breaking a world record.

From Tools to Toys to Tools Again

Slinkys and Silly Putty started out to be tools. But they ended up as fun toys. Children played with them. Later, adults found ways to use them as different tools.

- The Slinky is a teaching tool. Students learn how waves move.

- Slinkys were science tools. NASA used them in physics experiments during a space shuttle flight.

- Silly Putty is a cleaning tool. It cleans typewriter keys and picks up lint.

- Silly Putty is a plug. It can be used to plug leaks.

- The Slinky was a communications tool. U.S. soldiers in Vietnam used them as radio antennas.